Trimp
Tromp
Trump

J-P Voillequé

Copyright © 2017 J-P Voillequé

All rights reserved.

ISBN: 0692966528
ISBN-13: 978-0692966525

DEDICATION

For Carmen, who suggested this project,
and Claire, who thought it was awesome.

CONTENTS

Author's Note   i

Poems   1

About   104

AUTHOR'S NOTE

This book is the result of a writing project: during the first one hundred days of the Trump administration, I would write one poem per day about the orange interregnum. I ended up with roughly 120 poems when all was said and done. The chronology of this volume is slightly skewed as a result of sifting through and picking what I thought were the best one hundred poems of the bunch. This should hopefully feel normal for most readers, whose own memories have been savaged by 2017.

1.

One of the debate topics when I was a kid
(I don't remember the actual resolution,
like most resolutions made or witnessed,
like the silent promise to persevere
that we make each morning)

allowed affirmatives to run a plan banning
the importation of Mexican avocados.
The evidence for, and glowing forecasts of the success of,
the plan to ban the avocados
came from the California avocado board.

All of the literature produced by the California folks
was copy/paste from centuries old
anti-miscegenation rhetoric. Mexican avocados
were going to come north and impregnate
our pure, creamy American avocados

with an army of mulatto spawn. Taco trucks
on every corner.
Trimp Tromp Trump.

2.

The inauguration will have mineral notes
and a luscious mouthfeel.
The inauguration will be served with
a bechamel sauce and asparagus.
The inauguration's fifth chakra burns purple.

The inauguration will smoke a blunt
with Snoop Dogg and Willie Nelson while
Buffy Summers slays a vampire and
flies through the air after scissor-kicking off
the lectern, where Joseph Stalin's bible

lies open to Genesis 22 and that fucker
will take the wood of the burnt offering
and lay it upon the nation.
And the fire. And the knife.

TRIMP TROMP TRUMP

3.

He wanders
the halls
grabbing statues
by the pussy

/This home
could use
more gold leaf/
he thinks

Outside
millions
of women
rally

to the cause we should never
have neglected

J-P Voillequé

4.

The border is a sponge soaked in honey,
actual honeycomb in places where the bees
have created a squat for a tin pot princess.

The nation is a hybrid, absorbing, reflecting,
coopting, reforming. A ceaseless wonder
quite unlike your inaugural lies.

The people hold small boxes labeled "dissent,"
each identical, pulsing with a power
that must terrify you,

you in your new sheets and the weight
of centuries staring you down from every crevice.

The moon is waning, the nights deep dark.
You are the man who stares starkly out,
unsleeping, unsettled, growing rancid with age.

TRIMP TROMP TRUMP

5.

They passed a regulation banning regulations.
They brought back a ban on speaking.

They said the inaugural was a smash.
They said bitches weren't sh*t.

That mean white way we say it, like we
can't be bothered to form words.

They lied and lied and lied and lied
and lied and lied and lied.

6.

If I wanted facts I would've asked you.
I have keen insight, okay, into facts.
The fact is we don't know anything, man.
Who died and forgot to make me pontiff?

I have a keen insight. Okay, into facts!
The religious are mostly useful, though
who died and forgot to make me pontiff?
I'll waterboard 'em all if I want to.

The religious are mostly useful. Though
I walk in the shadow of the valley
I'll waterboard 'em all if I want to.
Noblesse oblige. My tie like a bandsaw.

I walk in the shadow of the valley.
The fact is we don't know anything. Man,
noblesse oblige, my tie like a bandsaw
if I wanted. Facts, I would have askew.

TRIMP TROMP TRUMP

7.

Any machine can
kill fascists. Pick one or more.
Pomes wrot wile u wait.

8.

Build the wall around Chicago
so that Malcolm's "House Party" can ring out.
Build the wall around Chicago
and blame Kanye.

Build the wall around Chicago
because Towkio's at the lake house.
Build the wall around Chicago
so that noname can have some peace and quiet.

Build the wall around Chicago
because those ladies murdered good men
over dumb stuff like domestic violence.

Build the wall, build the wall,
build the wall around Chicago
Because Chicago will come for you.

9.

As if art cares.
Let me tell you about art:
we made art before
there was money.

Art escapes out your pores
and boosts a car
and heads for the hills
with a box of sparklers
and a polaroid camera.

Don't get me wrong,
this is a nightmare.
But art? Art will endure.

Art will pick us up if we but attend.
Hang us from the rearview like dreamcatchers.

10.

You would turn away the Christ. Every border weeps,
Remembering the time before they were deified.

Adrienne is departed, but before her sweeps
the memory of ghazals, imperfect, left wanting

by this impoverished tongue, this pale mortar weeps -
it has spirit, and it tries, and fails to outlast.

The bricks have been lain too fast, sir. No more, yr steep
pillage through the lower alleys of America.

Ain't slumming. Concatenation of fascist creeps
has launched your ass into the big chair. You listen

at doors that open to rooms
named for men
who, without a drop of internet,
would find rage unknown at your cowardice.

TRIMP TROMP TRUMP

11.

We rise against false equivalencies
and the lure of simple answers
in a complex world.

In airport food courts we rise
to advocate for those whose hope is lost.
We rise for them because

every time we see this it becomes easier
to unbend, to stand,
to do our best,

whatever that best may be.
A nation afraid makes bad choices
and fine, disenfranchised white guy,

we'll get into your details in a bit.
Right now a Potemkin village is missing its strawman.

12.

Come lord Jesus, be our guest,
Donald Trump's a palimpsest

Yahweh, Yahweh, holy cow,
Donald Trump's a golem now

Mother Mary, help us please,
Donald Trump is made of bees

Gracious Allah, lend us aid,
Donald's nuked our Medicaid

Honored Vishnu break it down,
Donald Trump's a fat old clown

Hey Siddhartha, what's the haps,
Donald Trump is full of crap

Dear Confucius, time to roll
We gave the nation to a troll

13.

Dear Donald,

How are you? I just thought I'd write to let you know that the rain still falls. The sun shines in the morning, and the course of the moon and the stars at night move in the same way that one would expect for the time and the season.

The immutable laws of physics send their love. The infinite chasm of space would like you to know that your hubris is adorable. You are a speck on a speck on a mote on a dot in the universe, and not even destroying the world will change that.

But you go ahead and try, Donny boy. It's as good a year as any to snuff out this project.

Give the roaches my best.

14.

Panjandrum was a rocket-propelled cart full
of explosives but also
panjandrum is someone who thinks
they carry great authority and influence

and I am up late, single dadding,
and I can't not think of panjandrums,
or those who cater to their whims.

How Brad Dourif played both Piter de Vries
and Grima Wormtongue,
and how we live in Dune of the Rings:

merciless houses grinding their edges
against the wheel of commerce
while above them a great evil lurks,
and forges, and fears for his footing.

15.

The myth of the autodidact
is killing reality. There are no more
self-educated men than there are

pink dragons in the sky above the Capitol.
Yet we romanticize the self-read,
self-taught, bootstrapped, anti-intellectual

"I know common sense when I see it,
and the rest is just vocabulary" dude.
I met that dude at a party

and he was a blowhard jerkoff,
like the leader of the free world.

The hinges flip at the whim
of a man who thinks Frederick Douglass
is a living popular entertainer.

16.

There once were two racists named Steve
who wanted us all to believe
that whites were the best
and fuck all the rest
and our reps sit and silently grieve.

The Donald grabs girls by the vag
and wants an "I'm yuge" merit badge.
They fritter and fret
and seem to forget
they can take back the office he cadged.

The nation resists all day round,
in airports, at home, at impound.
We can't wreck it all,
but we can stand tall
and hope Congress extracts head from ground.

17.

Can you imagine Whitman
in the heart of this storm
watching his America
reenact the arguments
of his time
with weapons of such
phenomenal power and scope?

Can you see Uncle Walt
in the glow of his laptop
back-lit keyboard wet
with tears
as his captain, o captain!
subverts the multitudes
and "frees" the gays

by protecting the business community
that prefers to discriminate?
Not even consoled by the notion
that his beard is on point?
Not mollified by the sheer abundance
of wonder and beauty in today's songs?

18.

The men beat Jamaica
but it's the super bowl
so...

Donny kept gay marriage
but wants separate but equal
so...

F. Scott plagiarized Zelda
and had her committed
so...

We look and wait for the day
Dr. King dreamed of
but each day is a nightmare.

Each day the seconds fall off the clock
like the cherry blossoms, any day now. So.

TRIMP TROMP TRUMP

19.

The short list of better presidents
includes Gaga,
a can of Budweiser
any of the people
in the Coke ad,

Colonel Sanders,
Nationwide Insurance,
accented voices for your GPS,
any GoDaddy spokeswoman,

George Herbert Walker Bush,
both of his sons (sharing the office
so that they can figure stuff out

together), Barack Hussein Obama,
and of course Tom Brady,

Patriot, comeback kid, big blocky face
shining out from the machine.

20.

EOs anymore sound like orders -
or perhaps *ordure*,
call them the phantom lowing
of a dark slaughterhouse,

a handful of caretakers
whispering carefully in the gloom.
After all, Bayer//Monsanto
will grow the pigs on the trees

right next to the apples.
What is liberty to a pig?

21.

Teach the children mercy.
Teach exceptional people exceptional things.
Teach kind people street smarts.
Teach cynics about love.

Teach a new mother the things
that mothers know after a while:
that their child is different
(like every child);

that they will not break, even
if faced with gross cruelty
and indifference;

and that the lessons we convey
push the world ever forward
as they grow, and teach in turn.

Much is made of figureheads
and history books, and that's fine.
But right now, while we live
together here, I beg you - teach.

22.

In 2018 all the rural boys
will be Donald
& the urban girls
will be Persistence
(shortened to Percy).

They will meet in college
& occasionally fall in love
& hilarity will ensue
except in the many, many
cases of domestic violence.

& we will say the world moves on
& things change and isn't it
amazing how hate
can become
so
normal.

23.

One night at the courts on the UO campus
I met an ex-con who could execute
a perfect baseline layup,
floating through the air,
scissoring his legs so that
our suburban-born opponent called traveling

and the guy offered to demonstrate
that he was in fact floating across.
And here, Obama in his Jordan pose
heading for the basket

and I think that this may have been the first time
I considered privilege,
on a warm spring night with a guy
with previously poor impulse control

showing a useless player how to post up
so that the Beaverton dickheads
(who beat us)
would end up in a poor height match-up next time.
Dude lived for every next time he could get.

24.

Nothing we can do
will match what they do
to themselves. But.

What will they take with them
as they plummet to earth?
Porkington Trumplestein III

riding the nuke through
the upper atmosphere.
Also what they do

to themselves can't do
anything to love, or hope,
or #blackboyjoy,

or the sudden spring
pushing into your awareness,
the ice melting,

the sun on your face
like a valediction.

25.

Hey punkin,
rough day?
I couldn't
help but

notice that
your face
is haggard,
or more

haggard than
normal
because dude,
life is

misery
and pain
right up to
the time

you pass on.
Monkey
see monkey
do, Don.

Monkey see
monkey
do. You proud
monkey.

26.

Disambiguations for the confused:
Mara Lago is a Russian spy.
Mar a lego: to damage a Lego brick
such that it can no longer
be connected to other bricks.
Maral Eggos were invented
by a biologist
to boost the nutritional intake
of Caspian red deer. The nickname
was immediately slapped
with a C & D from Kellogg's.
Mar A Lago is where white people
can watch the deconstruction
of our security apparatus
while enjoying a daiquiri
and bacon-wrapped dates.

TRIMP TROMP TRUMP

27.

Shipping more than
Hannibal fans. Leaking
like the SS Minnow.

You let the football carrier
take photo ops
and you have the
audacity to be surprised?

Be my valentine, Donny.

28.

The parable of the man
with a stinky fish on his ass
is lesser known but apropos.

A man with a stinky fish on his ass
wandered into a border town and swore
that only he could solve the rampant
problem with armadillos.

The armadillos, to be fair, were not
top of mind for the townsfolk.
There were some around, sure.
But, said the man with a stinky fish,

the armadillos were in fact a dire
and terrible threat to the safety of the town.
You had no idea, said the man
with a stinky fish on his ass, just how awful

the situation of the town actually was.
Armadillos were responsible for
almost all the murders and 90% of the rest
of the town's violent crime.

People were like, whoa. But some folks
pointed out that it was challenging to trust
a man with a stinky fish on his ass.
Some funny math happened, and the man became mayor.

Once in the mayor's office, it didn't take long
for the man to stink up the entire place
because of the stinky fish on his ass.
No one wanted to work there. People who did work there

TRIMP TROMP TRUMP

ended up stinking of stinky fish.
The man with the stinky fish on his ass
grew increasingly incensed and desperate
for allies in his battle against the armadillos.

Anyway, it turned out that the stinky fish
was not merely on the man's ass but inside
his spinal column, and the man himself was
a dying sack of hubris.

That's the allegory - we are all of us
dying sacks of hubris.
But we can at least choose not to be ruled
by a stinky fish, or lizard people, or

good old-fashioned Russians.

29.

Doom foretold
on inauguration day.
No hope for
America,
less for our
deepest truths.
Just
two
racists, one failed
union,
mother Russia, and
parody.

30.

Comey's back in town, Donald,
and it doesn't look good.
It looks like a shit show,
if I'm honest. All this energy
driving you forward last year
and now, the let-off, the
actual weight of the nation
settling onto your restless
shoulders as you toss the
house, wander the halls, loot
the fridge as the night staff
watches appalled from a corner.
Honestly, man, I wouldn't
blame you for bailing. It would
be a welcome respite, wouldn't
it? Back in the boroughs,
lording it over the hipsters
who think they know what
quality looks like? Their logos
aren't hardcore – hardcore
is a gilt five-letter word
dropping like a bomb on another
country, all flash and sizzle
and, oddly, terrible food.

31.

An enemy of the people arrived at my door today
and carried wonders within itself,
spilled out in shy riffles as I gathered it up,
brought it inside to feed it coffee and crumbs
from my scone. Enemies of the people wake me
each morning and discuss pressing, interesting,
or just plain silly things as I struggle to rise.

An enemy of the people last night told the Donald
that he was out of his cotton pickin' mind
if he thought that the enemies of the people
would stand idly by as he lied, bald-faced,
to the people. We don't believe you.
'Cause we the people.
And our enemies are easy to spot.

TRIMP TROMP TRUMP

32.

We could just be a parliamentary monarchy
for four years. The Donald would
rant and rave and announce his greatness
and have rallies and parades

and all manner of bullshytt
and we could get on with the governing
and the application of laws and whatnot.
Of course, it would only clarify

the levels to which Congressional GOPs
are in the henhouse right now. More urgency
to defend the rights that are removed
whilst Trumples perpetuates outrage.

The glossy sheen of nonsense hiding
the dark center of the party's heart.

33.

I sometimes think that we
should never have domesticated cats.
Decorative fur throws all, but beneath

the veneer of tame animal
the claw, the hunt, the profound
urgency of protecting the home

against all foes. This last primal
trigger has blossomed everywhere
within our own monkey culture.

EasyD has us worked up beyond
endurance. Sanctuary meaningless.
The fire looms in the background.

Uranium, okay, it's a thing.
It's a really bad thing that is bad.

34.

Lord, let me never
descend to cynicism
when resistance will do.

Let me retain the lessons
of those less privileged
without being an asshat.

And most, lord, above all,
let me never think that
my experience is anything

beyond a single perspective
in a universe of light
and vacuum,

inaudible.
in awe, ya gulls.

35.

What's the deal with faith? What's the deal with discourse? What's the deal with pansexuals? What's the deal with modern art? What's the deal with O'Hara? What's the deal with Trump? What's your take on Cassevetes? What's the deal with Melania? What's the deal with liberals? What's the deal with conservatives? What's the deal with DC? What's the deal with the MLK Memorial? What's the deal with FDR? What's the deal with the new deal with the old new deal? What's the deal with art?

I ask you, what is the deal with art?

36.

At the end of "Robin and the Seven Hoods"
Sinatra is clearly clapping on the
one and the three.

Similes abound. Trump on the stump,
referencing crap he saw on teevee once,
painfully off beat,

waiting for adulation as his numbers
drop into syphilis territory.
Best wishes for a speedy recovery.

37.

As you struggle, I see you.
When you wonder if it's safe, I stand with you.
As you seek allies, I join you.
Much is made of otherness
as a hindrance to support

and I, top of the pile,
am guilty of failing
to cross the barrier gracefully
every time (or at any time)
but we fail and try, fail, and try,

and you there at the intersection
with the sign in your hand, with the tears
of thousands before you soaking
your clothes, I see you. I stand with you.

38.

The pool is full of lizards.
It's unclear how it happened.
We were out there with a skimmer,
the sun warming our shoulders.

It reeks of malice and spoiled meat.
The lizard talking points grate on the ears,
all hisses and sibilants.
The inner lids closing, opening.

Their flesh patched and scabrous,
they slither across one another.
Hardly room for the float chair anymore.
The seat occupied, lizards living the dream.

We are a nation of lizard brains
demanding recompense for the myth
that we were central to it all -
that we somehow deserved the best spot.

39.

In flags stitched over generations
rest tiny symbols of states,
places where citizens self-organized -
to a degree -

their existence within a given
arbitrary
line.
We say federalism

as if it's a sovereign specific.
A matter for the states.
Alas, matters for the states
cannot exceed the bounds of the

Constitution, which they too often do.
Jim Crow on forward, separate and unequal.

40.

I believe that reform is in order.
They drained the coffers before they'd
even stopped collecting the tax.

We're going to have nukes, big league
nukes, like a father's love. That big.
It's going to be like all the suns

in all the galaxies chorused just for him,
all the trumpets - so cruelly named! -
will clarion out in one last harsh scream.

We will leave smoke blots on the walls
of our cozy homes. And at least there
will be no talk of Obamacare.

41.

This is yr standard bearer.
A man who fails to respond
to actual events in anything
like real time, but who
doubles down on falsehoods
at any moment. This is the
plutocracy you dreamed of.

I would empathize but
I've never found myself
so desperate to reaffirm
a personal narrative
that I shackled myself
to a man made of bees.
Maybe in my fifties.

TRIMP TROMP TRUMP

42.

It's our own fault.
The man's name is
Jefferson
Beauregard
Sessions
the Third.

What else could we
expect? Could we
imagine him
to be free of
that weight of name
and upbringing?

Is there a man
alive more sad?

43.

Team-building for canaries
as the unbreatheable air creeps north.
We are asked to figure out
how to fit our troubles in a backpack.

"Consider the weight, the space,"
intones the white male efficiency analyst,
"find ways to delegate
or write your troubles onto another

and in so doing, emigrate
beyond a world where difficulty persists,
where your task list is a
pleasure cruise in a sea of Xanax and

forgotten
        shame --"
but it's too late and the voices ring
in the night. The brass-balled hubris

of thinking that we can talk out of this.
That there is a well deep enough
for the vitriol and treacle that
pumps endlessly from Janus' two pie-holes.
The spring of Lautolae, unburdened,
passing no judgment, scorching every part.

TRIMP TROMP TRUMP

44.

Ah to be emboldened by
the boring racism
of a world left alone
to its own petty nuisances.

To blow the whistle
and watch the dogs
scuttle out of their dark holes
to rain hatred

and baseless argument
on the next target of your
childish irk.
It must be delicious.

But the wolves, Donald,
are hungry and indiscriminate.

45.

Hard not to be a little depressed.
It reduces to this.
Grandstanding on conspiracy theories.

We are in the last days of Rome
and Nero is sat
in the corner, revenge 'bating

to a Sports Illustrated cover.
Not that one: no. One
with a wrestler on it. Oil shining

on his biceps. The Donald grunts
incoherently,
a furious pace. Nothing to do with

sex, even, just virility and
its discontents.

46.

I think Obama has wiretapped everything.
It explains so much about my xfinity bill.
What are these "taxes and fees" if not
tariffs on the surveillance state?

That's gotta be it, you guys.
How else do you credit this sudden
diminishing of our proud white franchise?
I was in a dither of concern
but now it's clear that none of this
is my problem.

It's that urban rabble with their
hippity-hop music, electing
one of their own and ruining
all this splendor for white men.

47.

I meant this poem to be about hope
but the Donald put paid to that.
Maybe this poem is about interwoven
egos fighting over scraps at the table.

Maybe, instead, it could be about
disappearances - Russians dropping
like colony collapse disorder
while Trumples whistles his way past graves.

Maybe it could be about calling
slaves immigrants and praising their work ethic.
I don't know, man.
Some days.

48.

Not a single day set aside, marked,
not a month. A chain of days
stretching from birth to death
in which gratitude is owed.

Homage to all women,
to trans women,
to women of color,
to women you know
and women you don't,
to the women in your life
and in the lives of others,
to the struggles of women,
to the triumphs of women,
and to the sad truth that
the two are so often
delivered in unequal measure.

49.

Seven weeks and it's harder
to care than ever -
what will it take for the apathy
to crack? For commuter rage
to mix with race/class/gender
and become riots at the bus stops?

But I hold hope like a skipping stone
in the crook of my finger.
You could mistake it for a white power
symbol but for the gleam
emanating out from the circle
formed by index and thumb.

For now we'll say it's OK,
this hope, this nest, these hands.

50.

To be so secure in your ignorance
that you don't pause
to notice

that the hashtag you're outraged
about is for
a TV show -

to turn to vitriol without a single
spark of curiosity.
To simply

dismiss for dismissal's sake. To be
the sort of person
who would

react first and wonder...later? Never?
Confess, reader: how nice would it be.

51.

Courage drags Statecraft
for not having the balls
to say it to your face.

Diplomacy has sunk so deep
into the bottle that,
were he a fly,

there would be no escape -
instead he circles the interior
on purpose, living on fumes.

Bureaucracy, ever the stodgy
hedgehog, plays the long game
with History in the corner.

They await you, Donny, though
you may not be able to pick out
their faces among the friezes
on the walls. You mistake them,
perhaps, for your father, staring
from your peripheral vision.

TRIMP TROMP TRUMP

52.

Molotov the bill of rights
except 2, expect 2 to
prove too resilient -
girls in tutus with twenty twos
and a dream of pointe shoes -

choose instead to enshrine
that one in a little box
on the desk in the oval.
Maybe make a label, quote Rove -
"all guns created equal."

Or the Gipper in a cowboy hat
from the glory days, man,
do you remember when we thought
that was impairment? Ah, Donald.

53.

Catching up with news anymore
is like "what fuckery today?"
Can't actually stand it.
Can't not do it.

Remember when it was enough
to get the New Yorker
and tut at the flyover states?
Remember when the big lies

were ours and sunlight was mostly
warm and welcoming
and there's weren't rats
the size of corgis

in the dark places that sunlight revealed?
Remember assuming things were fine?

TRIMP TROMP TRUMP

54.

No rehabilitating -care now.
It was the moment when the chords
aligned with Toto's flight from
the wicked witch, that I knew.

How else would expressions become
regular. Iterations on
shorthand, like Ashberry,
like ice forming in the Arctic sea.

You wander the halls ceaselessly.
It's the memory of your father.
Must be.

55.

They actually sing that champions song
before every game.
Imagine, Donny! Imagine if they'd
written a song just for you.

All the birds would be trained from birth
to harmonize with your song.
The most beautiful people would play
in the prison band, your song. Always.

Maybe someone would cross-stitch it
onto a square for a quilt - the melody
painted out in gold thread.
What a sight that would be.

Your anthem of hubris
in stereophonic sound.

56.

Ides, right? Big day for a leader.
Maybe not so much for you -
far more likely to impale yourself
on the Constitution.
But Snoop Dogg and the fight before
you - how dare he call you a clown
when you're so clearly a fool?
Not to harp on the nights, Donald,
but they must be lonely.
Surrounded by aides in case
you need a sip of water,
but alone nonetheless.
Others before you would speak about
the weight of governing,
but that's not your problem.
Your problem is the voices.

57.

The answer is more tanks.
Nukes will feed the people
with their radiant glow.
We will purchase small arms
and leave them scattered
across the globe to assist
the cause of peace.
There will be a slight
improvement in the condition
of those who serve our
country but not so much
that veterans can re-enter
with dignity
(they're mostly grunts after all
and would feel silly if
a fuss was made).

But bombs, boy, that's
something we can all
understand.

TRIMP TROMP TRUMP

58.

Trim the fat. Cut the umbilical.
Broil the poor and serve them with toast.
Put the elderly on the ice floes -
check that.
Put the elderly on rafts of garbage
in what used to be the Arctic Ocean
and float them off to true north,
where Valhalla awaits.

The glories! Canasta day and night!
A little nook for Trump supporters
to gaze at a photo of him at table.

59.

I can imagine getting stoned
and staying stoned
for the duration of this presidency.
If they were truly evil geniuses
they would let everyone
do just that.

Don't think for a moment
that these people
are good at anything.

TRIMP TROMP TRUMP

60.

Build the wall around Sesame Street
because the undocumented muppets
are the real problem.

Build walls around the courts
where the article threes hide
and say things that are hurtful.

Build the wall around Congress
because they can't seem to operate
solely on lies.

Build the wall in each of your
crawlspaces where dark conscience
seeks release

from the insistent peal of truth
occluding the narrative.

61.

So sorry Donald,
I fell behind. Your prattle
like cherry blossoms.

62.

On this day when sunlight edges out dark
nights and the evenings glimmer with rainbows
amidst the deluge we look up to the
heavens and speak, full voice: "The darkness fades
and here, you, me, all of us join together
at the table we made of this nation,
and we decide together not to take
this garbage anymore. We are bound for
a different democracy than the one
scraped off the bottom of Donald Trump's shoe."

Still we must, prostrate, plead for persistence
of senators, reps, average joes and jills,
child molesters, complicit murdering
villains, to remember the nation, the pact.

63.

I don't think God got this one right, Rex. It
happens from time to time that men are called,
but here, my man, the lines were crossed. Before
you rush to answer, think: was any man

less suited for the role of God's barker
than Donald Trump? Commandments ain't his strong
suit, any more than that man holding codes
is an attraction for fat whites at Mar

O Lago - o tempora o mores!
We shit where we eat and are surprised, nay,
stunned to uncover e coli in meals.
Best served cold, this grim reality. Rex,

digressions aside, we are in the dark.
The light you see is not your God's or mine.

TRIMP TROMP TRUMP

64.

When I was a boy there was an enormous guy
on my bus route. He was easily 6'4" by ninth grade.
Everyone was terrified of him, for decent reasons
(I believe he's dead now - a fight at a party).

We shared a bus stop, so my assumption was that
I was in for endless torment. But on the first day
of my freshman year, we were talking and he chuckled
at an observation I made about a comment he made.

That was that - I was insulated from all threats
(for the most part, it's high school after all).
Just by listening and reflecting back some tiny
thing, a thing I don't remember, in a conversation

with a guy who maybe felt a little underheard.
Suddenly I was all right. Compare to now -
one manic orange doofus whose glossolalia
contained enough meaning for the huge angry white guy

in our hearts to feel responded to and validated.
They were his from the moment he ranted about
whatever thing it was that was the last straw.
In that sense, we got the president we deserve -

the one who took the pent-up hate and stroked it gently,
said "I get that you're sad about the failure
of the universe to center you."
It's all they've heard from that moment.

65.

TGIF. The kitten's single claw
embedded in the twine,
its orange face a portrait
of distress.

Hang in there!

TRIMP TROMP TRUMP

66.

Down among the reeds and rushes
and organic sludgy muck,
the most nutrient-dense mud
from which to craft your golems.

It can't be this easy.
Is it really just a parade and
a round of golf every weekend?
You expected some late nights,

at least, and yet the engine
(you are assured)
is performing magnificently.
The unknowns are reducing each day.

We're reasonably sure it was Arnold
who wiretapped you - for Obama.

67.

Falling behind, Don
how is it that you are not
yet indicted? Boy.

68.

Only a witling - the basest gull -
would believe at this point in the nation.
The risk is substantial but loose,

like a roux turned to dumplings.
Too hot too fast.
He hit the atmosphere like a semi,

bellyflopping sideways, ripping
instantly, the foil-wrapped
morsel shredding and igniting

at the speed and the heat.
Miraculously, he survived that landing
and now stands in a crater

surrounded by sycophants and raccoons.
Obeisances scattered like lilies.

69.

Rural America cares about the big box
coming or going, about the jobs that
follow or flee, about the bathrooms
that the alleged virgins are exposed to.

Rural America thinks that marrying an animal
is silly. That laws that slip the slope
into that sort of thing are crazy. That we
just need to get back to when whites

did white things like get married and eat
Jordan almonds at the reception before
running to their cars to get home in time
for Murder She Wrote.

It sounds like I'm judging.
Rural America doesn't like that.

TRIMP TROMP TRUMP

70,

Vida passageira, man.
Pedro & Bruno have it right. We sit
in husks and ripen, color,
grow warm in the sun and elsewhere,
processes spin up that mean
our doom but now, sun peeks out
from ceaseless rain,
folks burning out their full spectrum lamps
and you, Donald, you okay?
You seem refracted in the shards
of our hopes. It's gotta weigh you down.
Maybe take a weekend. Hit a few balls.

71.

Why not now? Humans
had a good run, good numbers.
it's probably due.

We break forms, again,
instantly, before they can
even recover.

They ask "by what right"
but the question spoils mid-air -
who said they exist?

Who died and made you
pope? Who speaks? Whose song
is on the swift breeze?

Donald it's coming.
It's coming so soon.

72.

What in the world could be simpler
than signing your name?
It's everywhere, man, and you use
sharpies like they're
0.5 mm Pilots.
You would wield a Markwell
like it was a Sarasa,
purple, .7 for extra sass.

Phone phreaking it in all day,
EasyD.

73.

hey america do u think heaven was reserved
for whites who never tried oral
& won at least one ribbon at a fair?

do u think hell is so packed
with transgressors
that they're returning to earth
through a fissure somewhere in
central america?

is there a distinction to be drawn
between closeted gop paedos passing
anti legislation
& the 'corrupted' people being crushed?

asking for a friend who cannot speak
but lives in yr neighborhood.

74.

As a youth I was outraged
at the train car buried at Hanford
full of dead beagles who
were subjected to radiation tests.

It seems an unbelievably
innocent thing to hate, now,
and also like walking past the homeless
and worrying about their dogs.

They lie scattered across the globe,
victims of the endless churning maw
of capital and statecraft,
and our chief and his chief diplomat

have no clue how to respond.
Cannot comment, will not acknowledge.
I say to you: be angry about whatever.
Pick the fight you prefer.

But dear heavens, you must fight.

75.

neither fin nor feather,
it nonetheless swims or glides
across the consciousness
and whispers sweet lies
to those in dc's environs

your constituents think like this,
it whispers,
you're totally in an aaron sorkin movie
and you're the hero
and you'll get the girl

[replace sorkin with travolta
or noted ayn rand adapter
shorty mcneverlaid
for the rightmost]

TRIMP TROMP TRUMP

76.

So many museums in DC
and which ones will you kill
with an errant wave of your pen?
You're honestly worried
about your team?

77.

You can only have three foreigners in your matchday squad. You can only have three foreigners in state government. You can only have three foreigners in a company. you can only have three foreigners in your immediate vicinity. You can only have three foreigners in the bath. You can only have three foreigners in the fields. You can only have three foreigners in heaven. You can only have three foreigners in hell and purgatory too so Dante had better build a shantytown, in which you can only have three foreigners.
You can only have three foreigners per line.

TRIMP TROMP TRUMP

78.

We see the man get beaten
and dragged out
and I think "this is Trump's
America"
but I'm full of it.
This is the same America,
just louder.
The orange interregnum
is not the birth
of new racism
but the validation
of the old
and you there, with
a pair of thumbs
and a hatred of
injustice,
I bid you stand.

79.

Still behind but closer -
the pressure to endure
and persist is losing
to the ennui of this
much stupidity
in one house.

TRIMP TROMP TRUMP

80.

Nanchoff in the center doing Nanchoff things
and consider sport, Donald.
Consider the aspirations of tier 2.5 soccer
in your America. Mikey's as American
as they come. He's a whippy, compact player
who had a deal with the Timbers. He puts
his shoulder through the sternum
of a Cincinnati player in the thirteenth
minute. He just wants a time share in the Keys
and a coaching gig in twelve years.
Who knows if he voted for you. Probably not.
But he's a guy with dreams in a tough industry.
He's your guy, Donald. This is an American man.
You juked on every thing you promised him.

81.

maybe if we don't mention
the button, he'll forget -
not dementia forget
(though I'll take that)
but regular old "life
is busy and I'm out
of my depth" forget -
trusting to conscience
is surely a fool's bet

82.

If it were Donna rather than Donald
I -
I can't imagine.

This is a poem about failure.

83.

Build the wall around Toronto
because milk does a body politic
and anyway, syrup.

Build the wall around Toronto
because otherwise the Jays
will one day win the World Series.

Build the wall around Toronto
because Drake is stealing
hardworking American hip hop jobs.

Build the wall around Toronto
because Trudeau could kill a man
on 5th Ave and still poll better.

Build the wall, build a wall,
build the wall around Toronto
because Toronto will come for you.

TRIMP TROMP TRUMP

84.

Don's blem for real,
he might just say how he feels.
Nightmare rabbits are real, too.
They play the anthem at the egg roll
like it's baseball or something.

That's what threw you off, prolly.
It couldn't have been you wafting
into smug contemplation of
your phenomenal success.

85.

The peas came in regardless.
Shelling them is as it ever was.
The landscape so altered it's
easier to notice things
that are the same.
It's the time of year
that Portlanders go nuts
for patios at the barest
hint of sun. Yet, we
must count the days
on our fingers and marvel
at the speed of change.

I'm not sure there's a place for poetry
on the eighty-somethingth day.

86.

The forces pulling us are not
evil *per se*,
more a concatenation of stupid.
A confab on the stoop
of the log cabin
where honest Abe first swung an axe
or loved a woman or had a dog
or something.
It's hard, Donny, to know
which mythologies to weave
into your magnificent
fabrication (and that's just the hair).
I'm sitting here paralyzed
with laughter
at the thought of your library.

87.

You don't need health care
if you're living right.
You don't need protection
from the cops
if you're not a criminal.
You don't need anything
if you're a woman -
neither health care
nor protection from the state -
because women are magic fairies
who can visualize their own
well being.
Don't need taxes
if you're loaded.
They only get in the way.

Scarce days to go, literally
nothing to show.

TRIMP TROMP TRUMP

88.

State's a mess, Rex.
Are you just going to
steer the ass-end
of the ship with an I-beam
and a dream of the shore?

None of y'all are any
good at this.
You demonized Canada
for heaven's sake.

And I sit with a strawberry shake
on the one nice day
between the deluge.
River's high, Rex.
Fixing to burst through somewhere.

89.

Do you think
if you shake hands
with the pontiff
and you're, well, you:

that your bones will splinter;
that you'll immolate on the spot;
that the heavens will crack
with the fury of the triune God;

or, that the earth would just open
and bring you low through
the simple expedient
of refusing to support you?

You've woven a narrative so foreign
to faith, even Rome must sigh.

TRIMP TROMP TRUMP

90.

Makework for the interns:
identify things that we have
done more of.

Leave out golf trips - look,
you don't want to talk about
how much you're gone.

You don't want to make
this a thing. Sure, you read
out your plan and none of it's there,

Don, not a single bullet point.
But flurries of activity
have always carried you through.

This administration has more
swizzle sticks than ever before.

91.

We'll cut all the taxes.
Show me a tax and I'll cut it.
We'll spackle over the cracks
with discarded regulations
and a little gold leaf.
It's worked forever.

But the niggling suspicion
that someone's on to you,
Donald. That out there
is not a secret but an
intuition that you are
a lying sack of-

The infidels are back in your brain,
whispering rationalities. Cast them out.

92.

The energy of the streets is the same,
the little hints of spring reminding us
that this is all still here, despite
appearances, despite a certainty that
it will be gone tomorrow, the next week,
the week after the week after that.

It's almost 100 and you've not blown us up.
Well done?

93.

The privilege on this guy.
"I had no idea this would be
this difficult."

Donald you said that with your mouth
to a member of the press.
"I had no idea that if you

didn't do the job, people would
rally and protest and yell
spiteful things and think that
I'm dumb and anyway, I sell
real estate. That job is hard."

If only there was some way you could have prepared.

TRIMP TROMP TRUMP

94.

In six days it's 100.
In five days Sylvan Esso
and Gorillaz
and Feist
and lord knows who else
will drop bundles of tightly-wrapped joy
into the ears of a desperate populace.

I'll defer to them for messages of hope -
the long game feels like about a week
these days.

95.

Oh, are we revoking health care again?
No? Oh, it's taxes. Oh, no.
It's NAFTA? Really? Oh, wait,
it's the wall. Oh, no,
we're not building that, I guess.

Oh, you finally did the thing
where people can call in and report
crimes by immigrants.
In Portland this week
they ruled a police shooting
suicide-by-cop, presaging
the days of suicide by ICE.

By existing,
they endanger themselves.

TRIMP TROMP TRUMP

96.

The thing about humanity
is that tomorrow will evaporate
before the echoes are done
bouncing off the empty halls of state.
One thing's true, Don - this is
a dog & pony show. You bought in
hard before the inaugural
that was nowhere near as big
as your predecessor's. Maybe
you should have guessed then?
Anyway, buddy, you'll be fine.
I bet there's an Alex Jones
retrospective on some weird channel
somewhere. You could maintain
your coiffure for a good three hours.
Saturday will pass before you can
say "I am terrible at this, and I'm
even terrible at pretending
I'm not terrible."
In a way, you're gifted.

J-P Voillequé

97.

It feels like America should be greater.
Jetpacks, at least. The collective
disillusionment that we are not, in fact,
special, that each individual, and all of us,

amount to nothing much. We're grit
in a much bigger wheel. But people still learn
to spin a stone across ice while sweeping
furiously ahead of its path. Clearing grit,

see? Sometimes the guy comes out with
a dial measure to determine, in microns,
just how close a given rock is to the center.

You're nowhere near the center, Donald –
none of us are. It's the lie of progress,
brought low by the vastness of space.

98.

I don't stand by anything.
It is a policy I adopted
through hard lessons in
the art of construction

project management. Stand
by things and you'll get
killed. Things fall, they
drop from heights, they

perform erratically and
leap from the hands of
the person you were silly
enough to stand by. You

learned that lesson, see?
Don't you stand by me.

99.

Never, ever allow the histories
to drain the color from this moment. Stand
there, garbed in a suit from Indochine. Stand,
sir, while men of similar hues confer

and shrug, confer and shrug, tortoises and
dodo birds, jolly caucus race. Black folk
told you, Sydette says, and we can only
marvel that anyone could truly say

different. You stand there, sir, my lord, good king,
and we shall await your pleasure, cameras
in hand. In hands intent on holding those
few shreds of the flag we could gather. Stand.

It is the portraiture of darkness that
will lead us again toward some grey dawn.

100.
I was gonna write a song for you,
she sings. *Sing at such decibels that
all you'll hear is sound.*
She speaks to all of us and one of us.
Not one of us, reader, unless the whims
of some personified superstition can rally.
So amazing, to be the recipient of such a song.
Or the singer, really. To be the one that must
be made whole and safe and warm. We reach
in our finest moments to be that caring of
everyone, but we fall short, like those before us
but differently, maybe less often?
We each grow as we can into the shoes of our parents.
What, honestly, is nation to that? Sir Terry
would, I think, say "not too much."
The sun rises on the next hundred days.

ABOUT THE AUTHOR

J-P Voillequé is a poet and writer who also happens to have a law degree and wonkish tendencies. He lives with his family in Portland, Oregon.

ABOUT THE TYPE

This book is set in Garamond. The cover utilizes Porter Sans Block by Tyler Finck (@finck on Twitter, and on the web at www.finck.co).

www.ingramcontent.com/pod-product-compliance
Lightning Source LLC
Chambersburg PA
CBHW061334040426
42444CB00011B/2917